curious
creatures
stickers and activities

curious

creatures

stickers and activities

Anita Ganeri and Penny Arlon

weldon**owen**

weldon**owen**

Authors: Anita Ganeri and Penny Arlon

Design: Tory Gordon-Harris, Peter Clayman, Anna Pond

Editorial: Lydia Halliday, Susie Rae

Fact checker: Jenny Curran

Art Director: Stuart Smith

Publisher: Sue Grabham

Insight Editions Publisher: Raoul Goff

Published by Weldon Owen Children's Books

An imprint of Weldon Owen International, L.P.

A subsidiary of Insight International, L.P.

PO Box 3088
San Rafael, CA 94912

www.insighteditions.com

ISBN: 978-1-68188-741-8

Manufactured in China

First printed in 2020

23 22 21 20 19 1 2 3 4 5

Contents

Look for the fun activities in each chapter. There are mazes, dot to dots, word searches, sticker scenes, and more!

Find the giant poster and sticker sheets at the end of the book!

Curious Creatures

Some creatures have big ears, long noses, or huge eyes. Some have amazing shells and scales. Others are covered in hair, feathers, scales, or prickles. Some creatures have oddly shaped bodies, with incredible colors and patterns. Others have the astonishing ability to glow in the dark. There are millions of curious creatures on planet Earth, and billions of different creature features and shapes. A creature's appearance isn't simply for show, though—it is much more important than that. In the natural world, an animal's body shape has evolved over millions of years, and helps an animal to survive wherever it lives.

Some features, such as long arms, wings, or flippers, allow animals to move on land, water, and air. Orangutans use their extra-long arms to swing through the trees in their forest home. Birds use their wings for flying, while fish have fins and tails for swimming. Colors and patterns help animals to stay hidden, so that their enemies cannot see them, or they can sneak up on prey. They can also be a way for animals to send signals and keep in touch. Many features help animals to track down and eat their food. Animals that eat meat have sharp teeth and claws. Birds have bills and beaks specially adapted for eating leaves, fruit, and seeds, and for cracking nuts. Eyes, ears, and noses are essential sense organs for finding food in different places, and even in the dark.

In this book, you will meet a huge variety of curious creatures, from prickly porcupines and glittering glow-worms to sharp-toothed tigers and sea dragons shaped like seaweed. See if you can work out how their special features help them to stay alive.

Eyes and ears

Many animals rely on their senses of sight and hearing to find food and stay out of danger. Owls have huge eyes for hunting, particularly at night, and flexible necks that they can twist right around to look behind them. This owl's ears are on the sides of its head, covered by feathers. One ear is slightly higher than the other. The owl turns and tilts its head until it can hear equally in both ears. Then it can pinpoint the exact location of its prey.

Snail

Fly

Tokay gecko

Red piranha

Rabbit

Mottled garlic toad

Spider

Chinchilla

Koala

Crested gecko

Chicken

Sphynx cat

Lovebird

Donkey

Frog

Hen harrier

Yellow eyelash viper

Caracal

Ostrich

Garden dormouse

Dragonfly

Rabbit

Mandarin duck

Gecko

Bull terrier

Mouse

Snail

Flying fox

Red squirrel

Lynx

European scops owls

Jackson's chameleon

Hammerhead shark

Tiger

Beagle

Persian cat

Northern white-faced owl

European otter

Red-eyed tree frog

Fly

Australian shepherd

Blue-eye rainbow fish

Giraffe

Maine coon

Snowflake moray

Crowned sifaka

Domestic Pig

Dwarf neon rainbowfish

Caique parrot

Argentine horned frog

Common seal pup

Tree frogs

French bulldog

Red panda

Eagle owl

Friesian cow

Senegal
bushbaby

Longhorn
cowfish

Russian
rabbit

White
rabbit

Green
aracari

Shrimp

Hippopotamus

Border
collie

African
elephant

Telescope
eye goldfish

Indian
rhinoceros

Praying
mantis

Brown
bear

White tiger

Giant
pandas

Eye spy

Keep an eye on these animal puzzles.
They are watching you from all directions!

Follow the lines

The hammerhead shark uses
its wide eyes to find the squid.
Which path should it take?

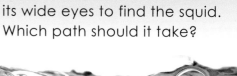

Hammerhead
shark

Seaweed

Squid

Seaweed

EYES EVERYWHERE

The chameleon can roll its
eyes up, down, backward, and
forward. It can even move its eyes
in different directions!

Sticker scene

How many red-eyed tree frogs can you find on your sticker sheet? Fill the forest with frogs!

activity page

Use your stickers here!

Maze

Can you help the eight-eyed spider through the maze?

finish

start

15

All ears

Animals with big ears have excellent hearing. Check out all the long, wide, floppy, and flappy ears in these puzzles!

Matching pair

Can you find the two identical fennec fox cubs?

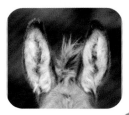

NIGHT EARS

This brown long-eared bat has huge ears! It can hear very well. Bats have the best hearing of any land animal, but not good eyesight.

Dot to dot

Connect the dots, starting with number 1.
Find the animal with the biggest ears of all!

Word search

These big-eared animals
are all in this word grid.
Can you find them?

s	d	f	k	c
m	o	o	s	e
c	g	c	w	l
o	h	a	r	e
w	e	t	w	v

Cow

Dog

Hare

Cat

Moose

Fur, feathers, and prickles

A fur coat can be vital for keeping an animal warm, and creatures that live in the coldest places often have the longest and thickest fur. Feathers do a similar job, and also help birds to fly. Fur and feathers can be waterproof, but need to be kept in top condition. Some creatures, like this porcupine, are covered in thousands of needle-like prickles or quills, made from sharp, hard hairs. The quills lie flat, until the porcupine is threatened. Then they shoot up, ready to launch a painful defense.

Chinchilla

Hedgehogs

Irish cob horse

Thorny devil lizard

Hooded pitta

Bactrian camel

Roosters

Rabbit

Caterpillar

Echidna

Chicks

Guinea pig

Angora rabbit

Macaw

Ducklings

Lionfish

Bee

Barn owl

Porcupines

German spitz

Lovebirds

Bullfinch

Zebra finch

Alpaca

Wild goose

Echidna

Sheep

Ferret

Giant prickly stick insect

Knob-tailed gecko

Pufferfish

Armadillo lizard

Rainbow lorikeet

Pied kingfisher

Mountain goat

Coypu

Brown bear cub

Llama

Japanese cranes

Andean bear

Highland cow

Shetland pony

Draft horse

Buffalo

Cockatoo

Raccoon

Snow monkeys

Swallow

Bactrian camel

Brown bear

Afghan hound

Gray heron

Hill blue flycatcher

Kalij pheasants

caterpillar

Wolves

Lion

Baby orangutan

Bee-eater

Polar bear

Buck moth caterpillar

Macaw

Ornamental fish

Bald eagle

Rhesus monkey

Husky

Arctic fox

Mountain goat

Shih-tzu

Fur and prickles

Some animals are furry and others are spiny. Can you find an animal that is furry and spiny?

Shadow hunt

The furry animals are looking for their shadows. Which shadow is missing?

Orangutan

Dog

Rabbit

Meerkat

Llama

SPINY SHOCK

When the puffer fish is attacked, it doesn't swim away. It blows its body up like a balloon and sticks out its prickles. Nothing will eat that!

Sticker scene

Use your sticker sheet to find the prickly hedgehogs. Add them to their forest home.

Use your stickers here!

How many left?

The furry, spiny caterpillars are hungry. Are there enough leaves for all of the caterpillars?

Feathers

Look at all the birds in these feathery puzzles! Birds are the only animals in the world that have feathers.

Spot the difference

Can you spot two differences between these two stunning peacocks?

FEATHERY WARM

Emperor penguins live in very cold places. They have thousands of waterproof feathers that keep them toasty warm in the snow.

What comes next?

Look at the animals below and work out which bird comes next on each line.

Use your stickers here!

Matching pair

Can you spot two feathers that are the exactly the same?

Color me in

Parrots have lots of different colored feathers. How many colors will yours have?

Patterns

The patterned coats of some creatures help them to blend into the background, hide from hungry enemies, or lie in wait, unseen, for prey. Some animals, such as chameleons and cuttlefish, can even change color to show their feelings and communicate. These zebras' striking black-and-white coats would seem to make them stand out in a crowd. In fact, their stunning stripes are useful for confusing predators who find it tricky to pick out a single zebra from among the others in the herd.

Wasp

Hornet

Sailfin fish

Pearl stingray

Budgerigar

Gecko

Clownfish

Giraffe

Butterflies

Blue poison dart frogs

Tiger

Malayan banded pitta

California quail

Wood beetle

Quoll

Mandarin duck

Snowy owl

Reed frog

Leopard frog

Starling

Asian leopard cat

Triggerfish

Cheetah

Blue-tongued lizard

Fresian cow

European turtle dove

Ocellated lizard

Royal angelfish

Harlequin frogs

Baby tapir

Royal pheasant

Cobra

Lynx

Lantern bug

Ladybug

Zebras

Fire salamander

Common
pheasant

Painted lady
butterfly

Asian
leopard cat

Orcas

Jaguars

Dalmatian

Okapi

Bengal
cat

Waxwing

Panther
chameleon

Jewel beetles

Flap-necked chameleon

Whale Shark

Sea turtle

Leopards

Pueblan milk snake

White tiger

Fresh spotted scat fish

Bumblebee

Alligator bug

Neon tetra fish

Bumblebee goby

Butterfly tiger moth

Lambs

Great mormon butterflies

Gray peacock-pheasant

Patterns

The animal world is filled with spots, stripes, and other colorful markings. Which pattern is your favorite?

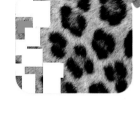

Word search

Can you find these patterned creatures in the word grid?

Bee

Fish

d	m	p	t	f
u	k	t	i	i
c	d	v	g	s
k	b	e	e	h
z	e	b	r	a

Duck

Tiger

Zebra

EYE SPOTS

When the sunbittern bird is afraid, it opens its wings. The patterns look like huge eyes and scare other animals away!

Help the giraffe

The giraffe wants to get to the acacia leaf. Can you help?

start

finish

Odd one out

Look carefully at the snakes. Which one doesn't match the others?

Draw the other half

Can you copy the patterns on the other side of the butterfly?

Beaks, bills, and noses

A bird's beak or bill has many functions—finding food, preening feathers, and feeding young, to name just a few. Beaks and bills vary in shape depending on what the bird eats. An oystercatcher uses its long, thin bill for probing mud for shellfish. A macaw cracks nuts with its strong, hooked beak. And noses aren't just for smelling either. This male proboscis monkey uses its very large, fleshy nose to attract a mate and warn off rivals. Its nose helps to make its honking call louder and more impressive.

Common
kingfisher

Blue
marlin

Toco
toucan

Hornbill

Tapir

Tree pit
viper

Green
mamba
snake

Sandhill
crane

Giant
anteaters

Sulawesi
hornbill

Spectacled
caiman

Rat

Jack
Russell

Chameleon

Koala

Emperor
penguin

Hedgehog

Nose horned viper

Cow

Southern ground hornbill

South American coati

Quoll

Hooded vulture

Giraffe

Hornbill

Needlefish

Emperor penguin

Collared anteater

Rats

Masked lovebirds

Aardvark

Longnose butterflyfish

Mandrill

Walrus

Rhinoceros beetle

Red palm weevil

Pigeon

Hummingbird

Guinea pig

Bay horse

Dusky hognose snake

Spotted hyena

Rooster

Flamingos

Wild boar

Argentine red tegu

Northern caiman lizard

Sea lions

Tapir

Ferret

Vipera latastei snake

Hound dog

Syrian hamsters

King vulture

Duckling

Hoopoe

Koala

Gambian pouched rat

Fox

Sturgeon
fish

Pigeon

Otters

Pig-nosed
turtles

Pigs

Hippopotamus

Asian
elephant

Malayan
sunbear

Sea
dolphin

Elephant

Proboscis
monkey

Bird beaks

Bird beaks come in lots of shapes and sizes. Long beaks catch fish. Thick beaks can crack nuts. Can you see a curved beak?

Which one has most?

These puffins have been fishing. Which one has caught the most fish?

GIANT BILL

The pelican's long beak has a huge throat pouch beneath it. It can hold three times as many fish in its beak than in its stomach!

Find the shadows

Match the birds to their shadows. The beak shapes might help you.

Hornbill

Spoonbill

Curlew

Kingfisher

Dot to dot

Connect the dots, starting at number 1. Can you find a bird with a beak as long as its body?

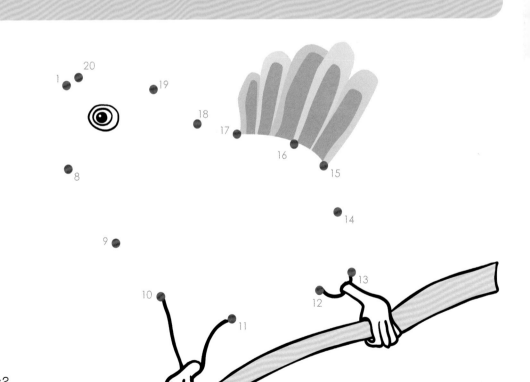

Noses

Get your nose stuck into these animal puzzles. Can you sniff out the answers?

Can you find?

The viper uses its nose to hunt animals. Can you help it find three birds, four lizards, and six mice?

SNIFF IT OUT

Great white sharks have an amazing sense of smell. They would be able to smell one drop of blood in a swimming pool!

Follow the nose

The anteater is following its nose to the anthill. Which line should it take?

Matching pair

Check out the mandrills' noses! Can you spot the matching pair?

Shells
and scales

Some creatures grow scales and shells to protect
their soft bodies. Crocodiles and lizards have larger
scales around their heads, tails, and feet, and
smaller scales around their joints. Other animals
grow shells around them—think of the seashells
you find on the beach. They are left behind by
creatures, such as cockles, mussels, and clams. A
sea turtle's shell is amazing. It is made from bone
and cartilage. This leatherback turtle is slightly
different—it has tough, leathery skin.

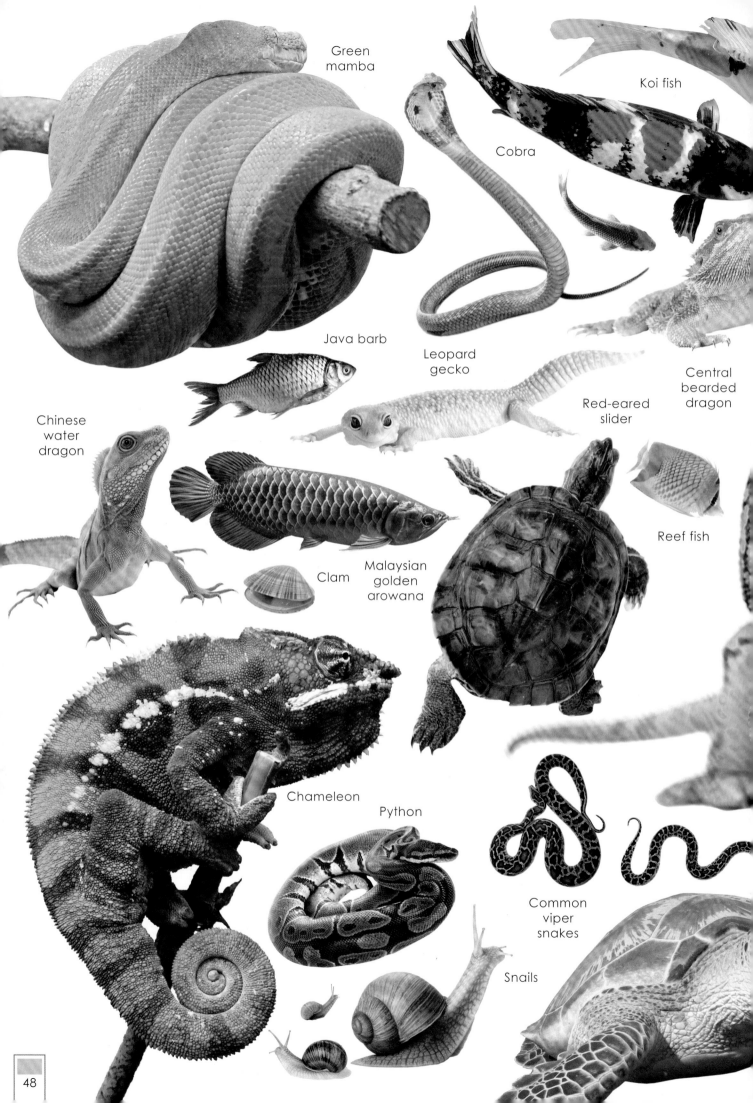

Green
mamba

Koi fish

Cobra

Java barb

Leopard
gecko

Red-eared
slider

Central
bearded
dragon

Chinese
water
dragon

Reef fish

Clam

Malaysian
golden
arowana

Chameleon

Python

Common
viper
snakes

Snails

Coahuilan box turtle

Field crab

Iguana

Rainbow crab

African spurred tortoise

Freshwater crocodile

Freshwater prawn

Goldfish

Veiled chameleon

Tortoise

Tokay gecko

Hermit crab

Loggerhead turtles

Lobsters

Whelks

Lizard fish

Blue tongue skink

Australian freshwater crocodile

Viper

Mussels

Goldfish

Aldabra giant tortoises

Common adder

Gila monsters

Yabbie Crayfish

New Caledonian crested geckos

River Crayfish

50

Oyster

Leaf gecko

Red-eared
slider

Garter
snake

Caspian
turtle

Fresh water
crocodile

Green
lizards

Sand
lizard

Siamese
fighting
fish

Corn
snake

Indian star
tortoises

Iguana

Blue zaire
frontosa

Giant
sulcata
tortoise

Grass
snake

In a shell

When these animals feel scared, they hide in their shell homes. Which have come out of their shells?

Sticker scene

Can you find the turtle stickers on your sticker sheet? Put them on the reef.

Use your stickers here!

A SHELL HOME

The Galapagos tortoise is so big that a 10-year-old child could hide under its shell!

What comes next?

Can you work out which animal comes next on each line?

Use your stickers here!

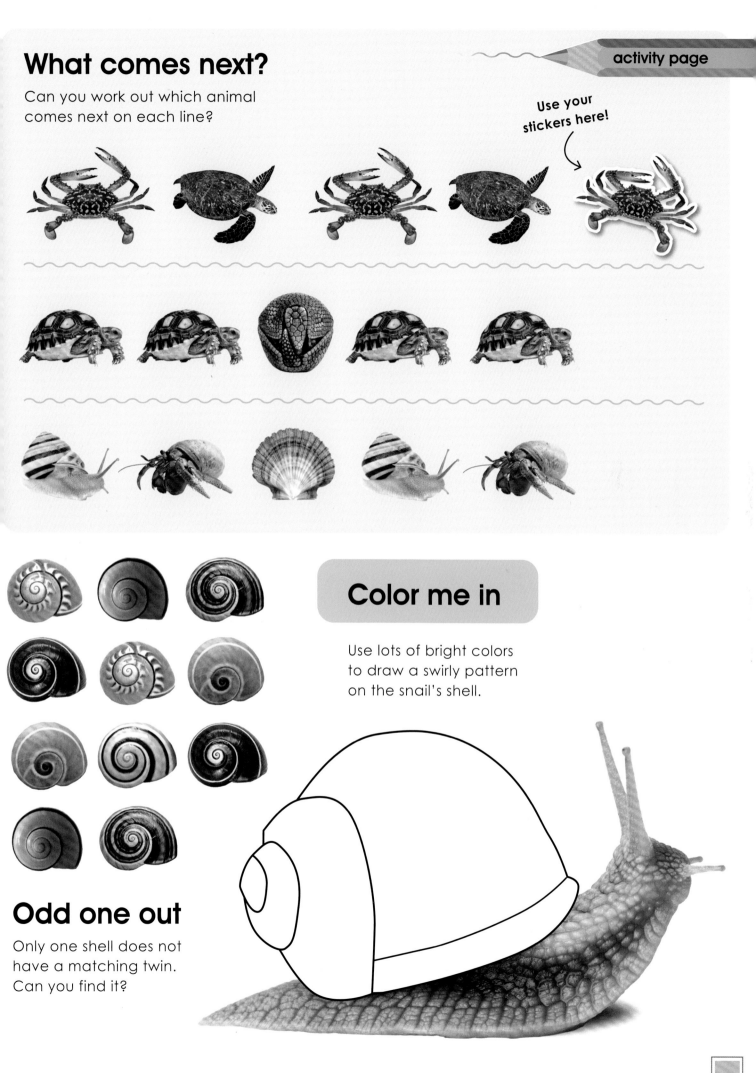

Color me in

Use lots of bright colors to draw a swirly pattern on the snail's shell.

Odd one out

Only one shell does not have a matching twin. Can you find it?

Tusks, horns, and antlers

Tusks are front teeth that keep on growing, and they're found in wild boar, elephants, hippos, and walruses. A walrus's tremendous tusks can grow three feet long. They're used for breaking holes in the ice, and hauling their owner out of the water. They're also a status symbol—males with the largest tusks take the top spot in the herd. Horns are made from keratin like your hair and nails, and antlers are made from bone. They're grown by creatures, such as antelope, rhinos, and deer, for fighting rivals and defending territory.

Longhorn beetle

Moose

Red hartebeest

Jewel beetle

Cow

Yak

Surinam horned frog

Banteng

Wood-boring beetles

Wild boars

Goat

Bull elks

Mountain goats

Flower long-horn beetle

Pipevine swallowtail butterfly

Rocky mountain goat

Arles merino sheep

Waterbuck

Greater kudu

Big-horned beetles

Ankole-watusi

Sika deer

Red palm weevil

Longhorn beetle

Flower chafers

Blackbucks

Red deer

Rhinoceros beetle

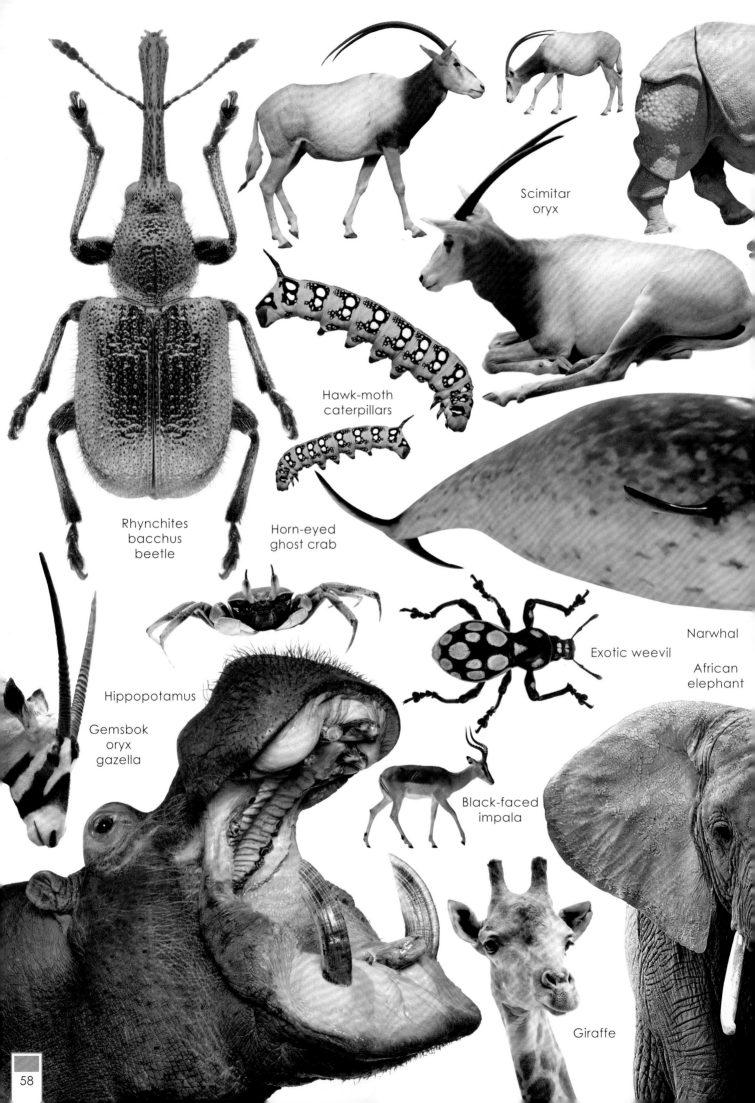

Scimitar
oryx

Hawk-moth
caterpillars

Rhynchites
bacchus
beetle

Horn-eyed
ghost crab

Narwhal

Exotic weevil

African
elephant

Hippopotamus

Gemsbok
oryx
gazella

Black-faced
impala

Giraffe

58

Indian rhinoceros

Gaur

Namibian springbok

Black rhinoceros

Asian elephant

Lanternflies

Impala

Nyala

Desert horned lizard

Stag beetle

Asian elephants

Tropical beetle

Dorcas gazelle

Mouflon

59

Horns and antlers

Look for the horns, antlers, and tusks in these puzzles. Can you spot the animal with the curly horns?

Shadow search

Check out the animals' horns and antlers. Can you match the animals to their shadows?

Chameleon

Beetle

Deer

Cow

Sheep

NEW ANTLERS

The moose has huge antlers. Each winter the antlers drop off and new ones grow in the spring.

Maze

The long-toothed narwhal needs to find its way to the shrimp. Can you help it?

start

finish

Word search

Find the animals with horns and tusks in the word grid.

r	s	g	t	f
h	b	o	a	r
i	f	a	n	o
n	l	t	z	g
o	k	u	d	u

Frog

Goat

Boar

Kudu

Rhino

Tails

As this whale dives, it lifts its tail high into the air, showing its two tail flukes. Underwater, it moves its tail and lower body up and down to power itself through the sea. Tails have many uses. They're used for brushing flies away, staying balanced, or gripping onto the branches of trees. Some animals, like dogs, show their feelings by the way in which they hold their tails. Ring-tailed lemurs walk through the forest, holding their striped tails high in the air. This helps to keep everyone in the group together.

Scorpion

Peacocks

Cat

South American coati

Macaws

Dolphin

Lizards

Gecko

Cottontail rabbit

Skunk

Earwig

Red kite

Cow

Ring-tailed lemur

Dachshund

Chameleon

Betta fish

Sugargliders

Orca

Flying lemur

Belgian heavy horse

Kangaroo

Zebra angelfish

Bay horse

Red fox

Egyptian jerboa

Chameleon

Guppies

Bell's dabb lizard

Siberian chipmunk

Armadillo

Pike

Pheasants

Blue tail skink

Barracuda

Rattlesnake

Koi
angelfish

Red
swordtail
fish

Marlin

Himalayan
bluetails

Turtle

Swallow-tailed kite

Kitten

Pig

Scarlet
macaw

Squirrels

Elf cat

Ryukyu
leaf turtle

Common marmoset

Sheep

Orange-breasted trogon

Shield-tailed agama

Manta ray

Senegal bushbaby

Crown tail fighting fish

Dwarf cichlids

Giant leaf tailed gecko

Blue moon lobster

Green basilisk

Western diamondback rattlesnakes

Lesser siren

Dusky leaf monkey

Sun conure parrot

Crocodile

Siberian sturgeon

Beaded lizards

Shark

Tail tasks

A tail is very useful. It can help with balance, swish away pests, and even grip onto branches. Which of these animals has the shortest tail?

Spot the difference

Can you spot two differences between these two flying parrots?

A NEW TAIL

If the green iguana loses its tail, a new one will grow back!

Find the bananas!

Spider monkeys uses their tails to swing from branch to branch. Which will reach the biggest bunch of bananas?

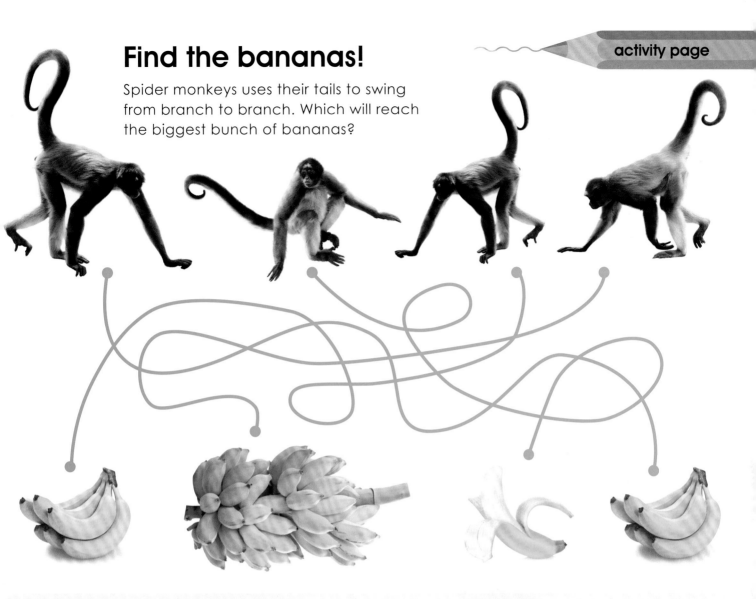

Draw the other half

How long can you make these vipers' tails? Draw them in and make them wiggly.

Body shapes

Curious creatures come in many different shapes. The shape of an animal's body tells you a lot about where and how it lives. Animals that live in the sea often have bodies that are streamlined for swimming. Animals that live underground are built for digging and wriggling through the soil. Some animals are shaped to look like their surroundings, for camouflage. This pygmy seahorse's bumpy, pink skin helps it to hide among its coral reef habitat.

Comet fish

Pygmy seahorse

Armadillos

Siamese fighting fish

Leaf insects

Moray eel

Sea star

Bird wrasse

Triggerfish

Pufferfish

Seahorse

Egyptian vulture

Ribbon eels

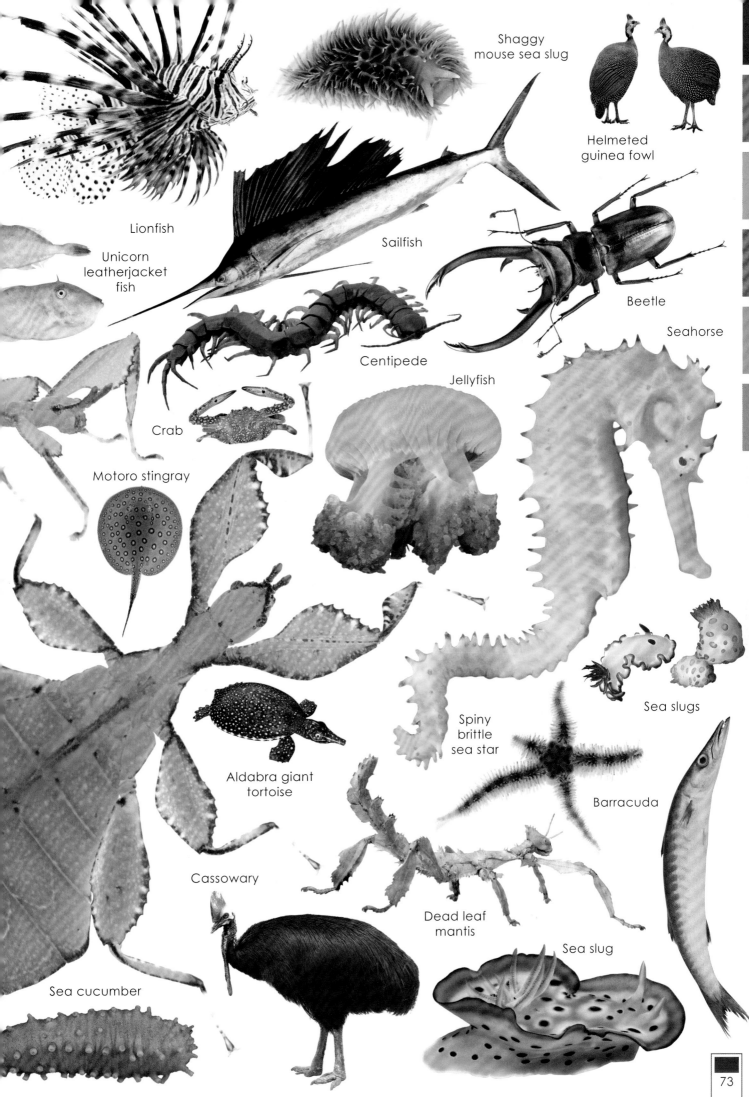

Shaggy mouse sea slug

Helmeted guinea fowl

Lionfish

Unicorn leatherjacket fish

Sailfish

Beetle

Seahorse

Centipede

Jellyfish

Crab

Motoro stingray

Sea slugs

Spiny brittle sea star

Aldabra giant tortoise

Barracuda

Cassowary

Dead leaf mantis

Sea slug

Sea cucumber

Flying lemur

Jellyfish

Octopuses

Leopard shark

Siamese fighting fish

Stingray

Shrimp

Saiga antelope

Echidna

Maned wolf

White whale

European mole

Lionfish

Discus fish

Mole cricket

Long-necked turtle

Portuguese man o'war

Flying fish

Shoebill

Axolotls

Stick insect

Triggerfish

Gerenuk

Goldenrod crab spider

Gila monster

Horseshoe crab

Prionus beetles

Crab spider

Armadillos

Komodo dragon

Shapes

There are some crazy shapes in the animal world. Look at all the different shapes of these creatures!

Find the shadows

Match the shadows to the strange-shaped creepy-crawlies.

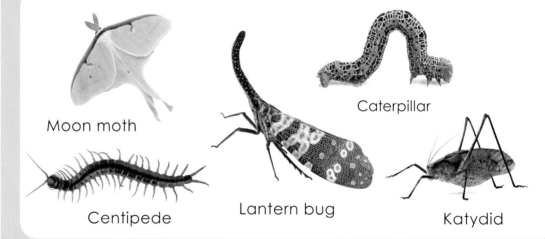

Moon moth

Caterpillar

Centipede

Lantern bug

Katydid

Odd one out

Which one of these curly pill millipedes doesn't have a matching twin?

IS IT A LEAF?

Leaf insects are the same shape as a leaf. If they need to hide, they just stay very still among green leaves!

How many left?

The spiky lionfish are looking for a piece of knobby coral to nibble. If there is one piece each, how many will go without?

Matching pair

Look at the six tall, slender giraffes. Can you spot two that are exactly the same?

Arms, legs, hands, and feet

How many legs does a millipede have? The answer is up to 750! Its body is divided into segments, with two pairs of legs on each. It uses its legs for burrowing through rotten leaves and soil. Other animals have limbs designed for running, hopping, and climbing. Gibbons' arms are extra-long for swinging through the trees. Some creatures use their limbs for digging—moles have spade-like front paws. Some have hands and feet perfectly shaped for gripping, or catching and eating food.

Malu
millipedes

Bonobo

Gibbon

Orangutan

Mouse

Bengal
cats

Lion

Poison dart
frogs

Greater
Egyptian
jerboa

Basset
hound

Great
Dane

Huntsman
spiders

Scorpion

Tree frog

Foals

Orangutan

Caterpillar

White-cheeked gibbon

Caique

Andalusian horse

Brown bear

Grey heron

Secretary birds

Kangaroo

Octopuses

Squirrel monkey

Crab spider

Somali wild donkey

Millipedes

Macaque

Brown spider monkey

Mantis

Orangutans

Centipedes

Capybara

Flamingos

California sea lions

Centipede

Gibbon

Tarantula

Otter

Cougar

Grasshopper

Lion cub

Chickens

Kitten

Flamingo

Sea star

Sea lion

Red-eyed tree frog

Brazilian galliwasp

Stick insect

Gambian pouched rat

Giraffe

Spurge hawk caterpillar

Prionus beetle

Jaguar

Raccoon

Blue-footed booby

Arms and legs

The animals in these puzzles use their arms and legs to bounce, crawl, run, and even swim!

Count the legs

Can you find two animals with eight legs?

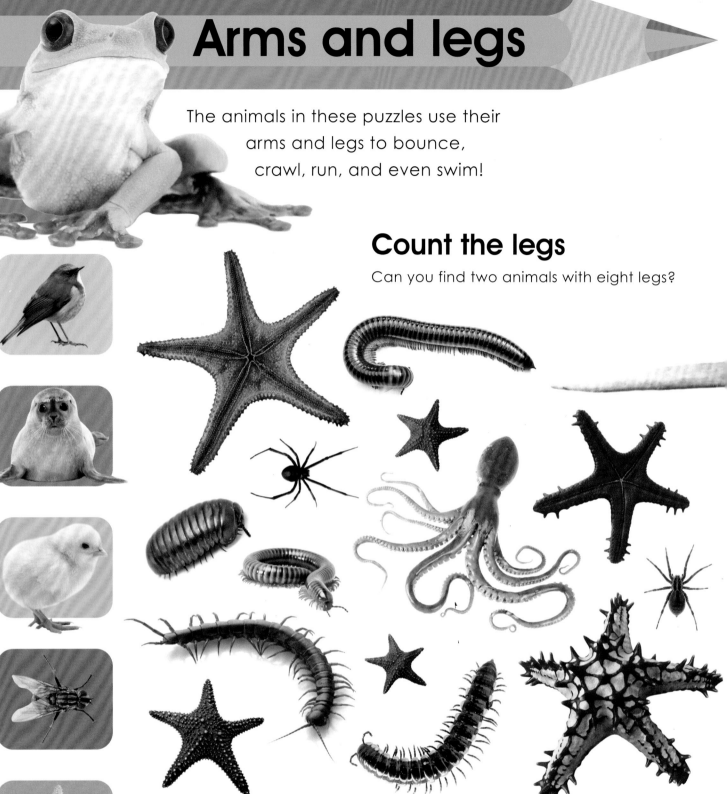

STICKY FINGERS

The gecko uses its feet to grip onto smooth walls. It can even run upside-down across ceilings!

Follow the path

The kangaroo hops on its long back legs. Help it hop through the maze to find the baby.

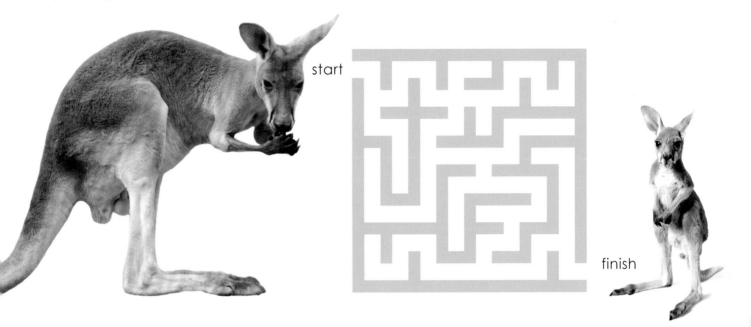

start

finish

Sticker scene

Find the long-legged flamingoes on your sticker sheet. Put them into the lake to search for shrimp.

Use your stickers here!

85

Wings

Birds are kings of the air, with wings perfectly evolved for flight. A few birds have wings but cannot fly. Penguins use their wings to "fly" underwater instead. A bird's wings may be different shapes—long and slender for gliding, or short and pointed for speed. By flapping their wings incredibly fast, hummingbirds can hover in one place. Bats are flying mammals. Their wings are formed from their hands and arms. Their fingers are extra-long to support the leathery skin stretched across them. This dragonfly flutters through the air on beautifully colored wings.

Butterfly

European
herring gull

Rose chafer

Brahminy
kite

Blue-tailed
bee eater

Ring-necked
parakeet

Butterflies

Birds of
paradise

Pigeon

Budgerigars

Owl
butterfly

Common
ravens

Atlas moths

Sea
eagle

Rooster

Wasp

Roller
bird

Macaw

Giant
rhinoceros
beetles

Hornbill

Hummingbird

Flies

Flying
fish

Milkweed
locust

Butterfly

Ladybug

Zebra
finch

Stick
insect

Eagle owl

Golden eagle

Goldfinches

Moths

Canada goose

Galapagos penguins

Hummingbird

Geese

Yellow bittern

Flying grasshopper

Bee eater

Bees

Parrot

Seagull

Barn owl

Peacock

Penguin

Alexandrine
parakeet

Red palm
weevils

Bats

Turkeys

Eastern
pondhawk
dragonfly

Wings

The skies are filled with flying creatures! Look for some fliers and flutterers in these puzzles.

Follow the lines

The goldfinches are after a juicy beetle. Which one will reach it?

FURRY FLIER

The flying fox is the biggest bat in the world. Stretch your arms out to find out how big its wingspan is!

Spot the difference

Can you spot three differences between the two butterflies?

What comes next?

Look carefully at the winged animals. What comes next?
Use your stickers to fill in the gaps.

Use your stickers here!

93

Teeth
and claws

A tiger silently stalks its prey through the forest, until it's close enough to pounce. It is armed with lethal weapons—super-sharp claws and super-sharp teeth—for catching and killing its prey. Animals also use their claws for digging, climbing trees, self-defense, and grooming their feathers or fur. A shark's teeth, like a tiger's, are designed for tearing flesh. But a plant-eater's teeth are wide and flat for grinding up plants. Some teeth have other functions—a viper's teeth have become fearsome fangs for injecting poison.

Brown-patched kangaroo lizard

Blue crabs

Snake

Bluethroat bird

Scorpions

Prairie dog

North American beavers

Plumed basilisks

White tiger cub

Cassowary

American bald eagle

Crayfish

Crocodile

Tiger

Fiddler crab

Chick

Bat

Lion cubs

Eagle

Cat

Crocodile

Piranha fish

Brown bear

Wattled jacana birds

Hippopotamuses

Book scorpion

Eagle owl

Little owl

Polar bears

Lion

Lamprey fish

Collie

Skunk

Field crabs

Blue crayfish

African clawed frogs

Saarloos wolfdog

Spider crabs

Macaque

Crayfish

Two-toed
sloth

British
shorthair
cat

Hawk

Zebra

Iguana

Panda

Horse

Small tufted
deer

Razor-sharp teeth

Quick! Get your teeth into these puzzles before they start to snap, chomp, and bite!

Squid

Turtle

Tuna

Crab

Shadow search

The sharp-toothed tiger shark is hunting. Look at the shadow. Which sea creatures has it found?

SUPER-TEETH!

Rabbits' teeth never stop growing! When the rabbits chew, it wears the teeth down and stops them getting too long.

Odd one out

Which snappy crocodile does not match the others?

Word search

Can you find these toothy animals in the word grid?

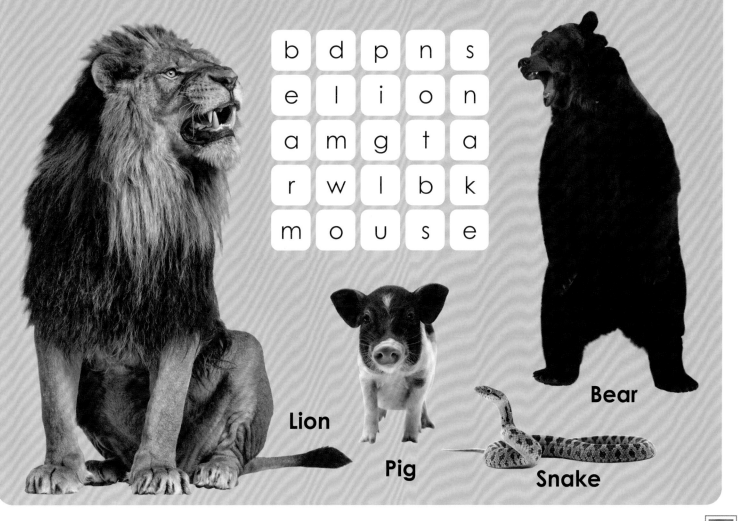

Mouse

b	d	p	n	s
e	l	i	o	n
a	m	g	t	a
r	w	l	b	k
m	o	u	s	e

Lion

Pig

Snake

Bear

Tearing claws

Animals use their sharp claws to grab things and to help them climb. Watch out for the claws in these puzzles!

Dot to dot

Connect the dots, starting with number 1. Which animal do the long claws belong to?

CLAWS OUT!

Tigers have extremely sharp, huge claws. Each claw is the length of your hand!

How many left?

The pandas use their claws to climb bamboo canes and eat the leaves. Are there enough leaves for all the pandas?

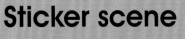

Sticker scene

Can you find the eagles on your sticker sheet? Add them to the scene.

Use your stickers here!

Glow in the dark

Some curious creatures, in the sea and on land, are able to make their own light—a wonder of the natural world. They may live in places, like the darkest depths of the sea, where there is little light, or only come out at dusk. They use their lights to attract prey, camouflage themselves, frighten attackers, or send signals. Glow-worms flash their lights in the darkness to attract mates. Each species has its own pattern of flashes that allows individuals to recognize each other. These jellyfish create their own light using a process called "bioluminescence."

Fireflies

Jellyfish

Bioluminescent algae

Larval tube anemone

Comb jellyfish

Japanese sea
nettle jellyfish

Sea slugs

Jellyfish

Filefish

Glowworm

Crystal jellyfish

Bioluminescent
mushrooms

Moon jellyfish

Click beetle

Bioluminescent
scorpion

Copepods

Comb jelly

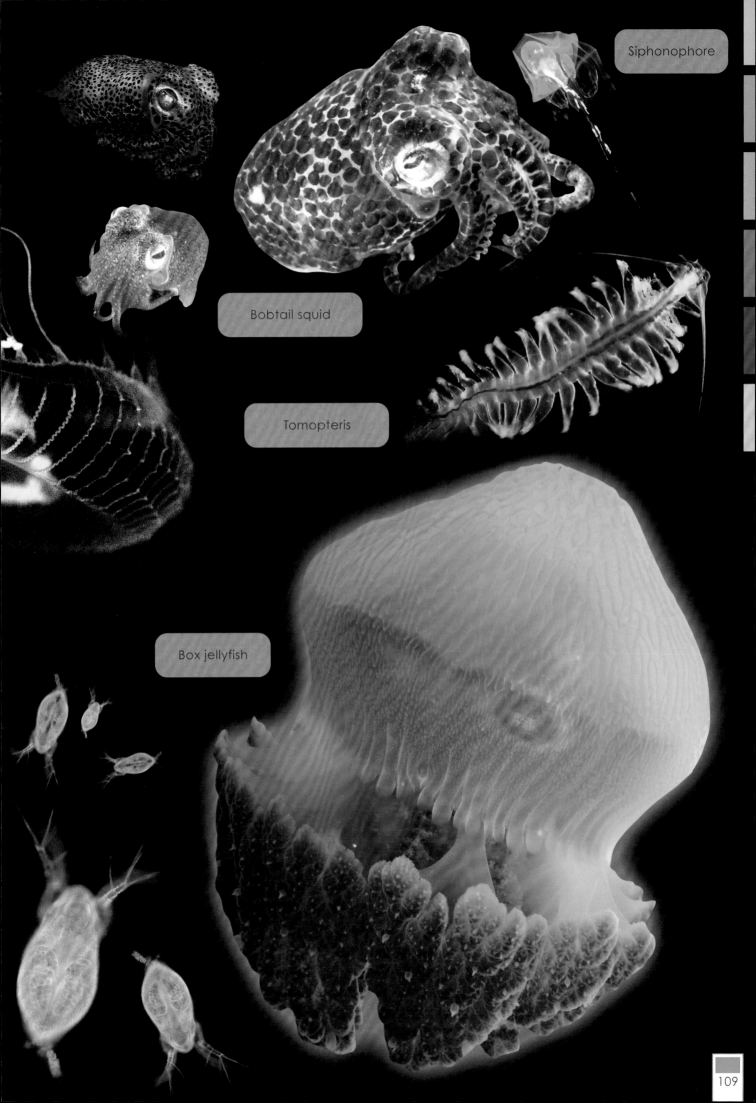

Siphonophore

Bobtail squid

Tomopteris

Box jellyfish

Glow in the dark

Some animals can make their own light. They shine and flash to send messages to each other.

Matching pair

Look at the twinkling jellyfish. Can you find a matching pair?

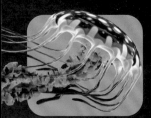

LIGHT SHOW

The blue-ringed octopus makes flashing patterns with its lights. It uses its flashes to warn predators to go away.

Maze

The flashing squid is trying to find its friends. Can you help it?

start

finish

Follow the lines

The glowing fireflies are flying towards lights. Which one will reach its friend?